LGBTQIA+

Written by
William Anthony

Designed by
Danielle Rippengill

LGBTQIA+© 2024 BookLife Publishing.
This edition is published by arrangement with BookLife Publishing.

North American adaptation copyright © 2025 by North Star Editions, Mendota Heights, MN 55120. All rights reserved. No part of this book may be reproduced or utilized in any form or by any means without written permission from the publisher.

sales@northstareditions.com | 888-417-0195

Library of Congress Control Number:
2024945366

ISBN
979-8-89359-260-3 (library bound)
979-8-89359-268-9 (paperback)
979-8-89359-276-4 (epub)
979-8-89359-283-2 (hosted ebook)

Printed in the United States of America
Mankato, MN
012025

Written by:
William Anthony

Edited by:
Robin Twiddy

Designed by:
Danielle Rippengill

All facts, statistics, web addresses, and URLs in this book were verified as valid and accurate at time of writing. No responsibility for any changes to external websites or references can be accepted by either the author or publisher.

Image Credits

All images are courtesy of Shutterstock.com, unless otherwise specified. With thanks to Getty Images, Thinkstock Photo and iStockphoto. Cover – Svetlosila, Zenstockers, rosewind, ursulamea, GoodStudio. Images used on every page – Svetlosila, rosewind, ursulamea. 2 – GoodStudio. 4&5 – Anatoliy Karlyuk, Halfpoint, M_Agency, SeventyFour. 6&7 – Lakkana Boonrat, NadyGinzburg, PARALAXIS, Patrick Foto. 8&9 – Antonello Marangi, Daniele COSSU, dominika zara, GoodStudio. 10&11 – DisobeyArt, Halfpoint, wavebreakmedia, GoodStudio. 12&13 – John Cairns, CC BY 4.0 <https://creativecommons.org/licenses/by/4.0>, via Wikimedia Commons, Ben Warwick-Champion, Ron Adar, GoodStudio. 14&15 – fizkes, Joe Ferrer, wavebreakmedia, GoodStudio. 16&17 – Dennis Wegewijs, Fabian Plock, Joseph Sohm, By The-time-line - Own work, CC BY-SA 3.0, GoodStudio. 18&19 – Rawpixel.com, Rupert Rivett, Syda Productions, GoodStudio. 20&21 – Boxed Lunch Production, soft_light, tonyzhao120, GoodStudio. 22&23 – KlingSup, Lemon Tree Images, Syda Productions, GoodStudio. 24&25 – StudioSmart, wavebreakmedia, Greenbangalore, CC BY-SA 4.0 <https://creativecommons.org/licenses/by-sa/4.0/>, via Wikimedia Commons, GoodStudio. 26&27 – Ellyy, Hajakely, Stock-Asso, GoodStudio. 28&29 – 24K-Production, POP-THAILAND, GoodStudio.

CONTENTS

Page 4	Being Brave
Page 6	LGBTQIA+
Page 10	Laverne Cox
Page 12	Write a Script
Page 14	Arsham Parsi
Page 16	Help Others
Page 18	Kian Tortorello-Allen
Page 20	Get Social
Page 22	Bayard Rustin
Page 24	Peaceful Protest
Page 26	Edith Windsor
Page 28	My Name Is Brave
Page 30	Glossary
Page 32	Index

LOVE IS LOVE

WORDS THAT LOOK LIKE this ARE EXPLAINED IN THE GLOSSARY ON PAGE 30.

BEING BRAVE

What do you think being brave means? Does it mean not being afraid of things? Is it when you don't put your hands over your eyes when there's a spooky show on TV? Is it when you are not terrified of a roller coaster with a giant loop? **NO!**

Nothing frightens me!

Who is the bravest person that you know?

Being brave is about being scared to do something, but still doing it because you know you need to. It is about standing up for people and ideas even when you are nervous or frightened to.

Activism

Making big changes in the world can seem scary. Some people might not like what you say. Other people might try to stop you. Activists are people who bravely speak out about things they think need to change. They want to help the world.

Making a Change

There are lots of different ways to be an activist. Many activists take part in protests. Others might make a speech to lots of people. Today, lots of activists try to tell people about their ideas online.

LGBTQIA+

When someone asks you about what makes you who you are, it can be tough to answer. What would you say? For many people, it is about the things they enjoy, who they **aspire** to be like, and what they do every day.

What if you were told you that you couldn't be you? That sounds like an odd idea. However, for some people, this happens. Many people who are part of the LGBTQIA+ **community** have been told that they are not allowed to be who they are. In some places it was even **illegal**. In many places, it still is.

THIS IS WHY LOTS OF ACTIVISTS ARE TRYING TO CHANGE THE WAY THE LGBTQIA+ COMMUNITY IS TREATED!

What Does LGBTQIA+ Mean?

The letters in LGBTQIA+ mean a number of different things about sex, sexuality, and gender identity.

Sex

A person's sex can mean the **biological sex** they were **assigned** at birth, or it could be the sex they **identify** with.

Sexuality

Sexuality has to do with a person's sexual identity. This means the ways a person may or may not feel **attracted** to different types of people.

Gender Identity

Gender identity is somebody's idea of how they are **masculine**, **feminine**, a mixture of both, or neither.

The Letters

There are many versions of the LGBTQIA+ letters that people may use. As we learn more about sex, sexuality, and gender, more letters can be added.

LGBT

Lesbian: This is a woman who is only attracted to other women.

Bisexual: This describes someone who is attracted to more than one gender.

Gay: This describes someone who is only attracted to people of the same gender as them.

Transgender: This describes someone whose gender identity is different from the biological sex they were assigned at birth.

Queer: Someone may see themselves as queer if their sexual or gender identities are anything other than **heterosexual** or **cisgender**.

Asexual: This describes someone who does not feel sexually attracted to any sex or gender.

YOU WILL OFTEN SEE A RAINBOW FLAG TOGETHER WITH THE LGBTQIA+ COMMUNITY. IT REPRESENTS HOW EVERYONE IS DIFFERENT, UNIQUE, AND BEAUTIFUL.

Intersex: This describes someone who is born with a mixture of **sex characteristics** that are seen as male and female, such as **genitals** and **chromosomes**.

Plus: This is used to include all the letters that are missing from LGBTQIA. This makes everyone feel included. This can include people who are **pansexual** or **gender fluid**.

LAVERNE COX

Laverne Cox knew for a long time that her gender identity was different from the one she was assigned when she was born. When she was in college, she began her **transition**.

Laverne was learning about the performing arts in college. She went on to become famous for her acting. **Representation** is just as important as acting for Laverne.

10

Being a transgender woman, Laverne started performing in many transgender roles. It was important to her to increase visibility of transgender people. Visibility is how well a group of people can be seen in and by society.

Laverne has been breaking down barriers for transgender people for years. She used her fame to start speaking out for LGBTQIA+ rights. If people did not like what she said, her career could have been ruined. Speaking out when it is hard to is very brave.

IN 2014, LAVERNE BECAME THE FIRST TRANSGENDER PERSON TO BE NOMINATED FOR AN Emmy AWARD.

WRITE A SCRIPT

So, why exactly does visibility in the **media** matter? When a community is seen often in the media, other people are able to understand that community better. We can see how they live, their daily experiences, and the difficulties they face.

Visibility must happen in the right way. It is important to show the **reality** of a community's daily life. Sometimes, people can be represented in a stereotypical way. A stereotype is an unfair or untrue belief about all the people in a certain group. It is very important that stereotypes are not part of a group's visibility in the media.

TV Time

Laverne Cox is famous for her roles on TV. These roles have increased visibility of the transgender community. Let's write a short TV script with visibility in mind.

ONE

Think about who will be represented in your TV show. Maybe you'll include a transgender character?

TWO

Think of a situation they could be in. Maybe it could be a detective show? What about a comedy show?

THREE

Write what your characters will say to one another in the first part of the show.

Your script should include a character from the LGBTQIA+ community, but it doesn't have to be about them being part of the community. What matters is that they are represented.

ARSHAM PARSI

In some countries, being gay is against the law. That means it is illegal for gay people to be who they are. Arsham Parsi was born in Iran. He started being an activist for LGBTQIA+ people in Iran by starting online groups for them in 2004.

In 2005, Arsham had to escape his own country because of what he was doing. He went to Turkey. He worked very hard to raise **awareness** of the difficulties that LGBTQIA+ people in Iran were facing.

PRIDE PARADE IN TURKEY

Eventually, Arsham was accepted into Canada. Arsham was finally able to talk publicly about who he was and what he was doing to help LGBTQIA+ people in Iran.

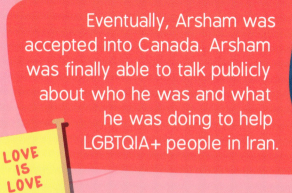

Arsham also started his own charity called the International Railroad for Queer Refugees. It helps people from the LGBTQIA+ community find places to live after they have escaped from their home country.

Arsham was extremely brave in a dangerous situation. He knew he could be arrested for what he was doing, but he believed it was right to stand up for people in the LGBTQIA+ community.

HELP OTHERS

The work that Arsham Parsi's charity does is very important. It is always good to help other people, but helping people who desperately need it is even more important.

HAVE YOU EVER BEEN PART OF A CHARITY EVENT?

Charities need to raise money to help people. They might get **donations** from people, or they might host a big event. Some charities host things such as bake sales or raffles. The money raised goes to helping the people who need it most.

BAKE SALE TODAY!

Set up an event

Let's get **inspired** by Arsham's charity work and set up an event to raise money!

ONE
First, you need to choose a charity to raise money for. Speak to a grown-up about who you might choose.

TWO
Choose your event! Will you bake sweets to sell? What about a **sponsored** race?

THREE
Tell people about it. You could make a poster to put up at school!

FOUR
Collect the money people have donated on the day, and get a grown-up to help you donate it to the charity.

KIAN TORTORELLO-ALLEN

Growing up is difficult. School is tough, parents can be annoying, and on top of that, you are discovering who you are and who you want to be.

During his time at high school, Kian Tortorello-Allen decided to tell people he was a gay transgender boy. Kian felt he needed to stand up for who he was and what he believed in. He was bullied for what he told people about himself. Sometimes, people bully others because they don't fully understand them or because they don't accept them. Bullying is never OK.

When Kian was at school, he worked hard to make it a more accepting place for members of the LGBTQIA+ community, especially transgender people of color. He also tried to represent people who were struggling and made sure their voices were heard on social media, where he could reach lots of people.

Kian was incredibly brave to come out as gay and transgender while he was just a teenager. He was even more brave to keep trying to make the world a better place after he was bullied for doing so.

GET SOCIAL

Kian uses social media to help spread positivity. Social media is one way of helping community members interact with one another. It can reach people all over the world.

YOU MUST BE 13 YEARS OLD TO JOIN MOST SOCIAL MEDIA SITES. ASK A GROWN-UP IF YOU HAVE ANY QUESTIONS ABOUT SOCIAL MEDIA.

Some people, like Kian, set up accounts and pages that help people find other people just like them. Social media communities can support one another and start important discussions about the things that affect them.

Design an Account

Even if we're not old enough to start a social media account, we can still design one! Here's how to start...

ONE

Choose your audience. This is who your page will be made for. Will it be the LGBTQIA+ community?

TWO

Choose an account name. Start it with an @ symbol.

THREE

Draw a logo for the account on some paper. Try to make it something that represents your audience and message.

FOUR

Design your first post! You'll need a photo and something that you want to write. What will you say?

BAYARD RUSTIN

Bayard Rustin lived in the United States during a difficult time. Black people were treated very badly during his lifetime. Bayard didn't let that stop him from standing up against the unfairness Black people were experiencing.

Bayard was good friends with Martin Luther King Jr. Together, they organized lots of peaceful protests. These are protests where no one is violent and nobody causes any damage. These events helped bring Black people together to support one another.

ONE OF THE MARCHES BAYARD RUSTIN HELPED ORGANIZE

Bayard was an openly gay man. At the time, it was not safe to be openly gay in the United States. People who supported the LGBTQIA+ community were also treated very badly. This meant that, often, the things Bayard did for Black people in the United States were not talked about.

Being both Black and gay made life very difficult and unsafe for Bayard. It might have been easier to hide that he was gay, or not protest the treatment of Black people. However, he was brave enough to protest because he believed it was important.

LOVE IS LOVE

PEACEFUL PROTEST

PEACEFUL PROTEST

Protests are a type of event where people gather in a particular place to demand a change. Protesters are usually trying to make the world a better place. Most protests are peaceful, like Bayard Rustin's.

Sometimes, protests can get out of control. People's emotions can become too strong, and the protest can turn dangerous or violent. It is always important to try to protest peacefully.

VIOLENT PROTEST

Keep the Peace

What in the world would you change if you could? Let's pretend we are organizing a peaceful protest!

ONE

Choose something you would like to change. This is called your mission statement. Maybe it could be something about how people are being treated?

TWO

Decide on a place for your protest to take place. Make sure it is safe for everyone. Maybe you could choose somewhere that is important for your message?

THREE

Tell people about your protest! Maybe you could make a poster with the information on it?

EDITH WINDSOR

For a long time in the United States, same-sex couples did not have the same opportunities as heterosexual couples. They could not even marry each other. Edith Windsor faced this problem herself.

Edith was in a lesbian relationship for more than 40 years. She could not get married in the United States. So, in 2007, she traveled to Canada with her partner to get married there instead.

Edith's wife died in 2009. When someone in a marriage dies, the other person does not have to pay **taxes** on the money they leave behind. Because the United States did not recognize same-sex marriages at this time, Edith had to pay a huge amount of money in taxes.

Edith decided to sue the government for its unfair laws. Not only did she win, but she opened the door for same-sex marriages to be made legal in the United States in 2015! Now, anyone can get married to anyone there.

MY NAME IS BRAVE

Anyone can change something for the better. Whether or not you are someone famous like the people in this book, you can make a difference. You just need to believe that you can.

Asking for a change that can make the lives of the LGBTQIA+ community better and safer might look like a big task. Some people might not like what you say. Other people might try to make it hard for you to change things. Do your best not to listen to those people.

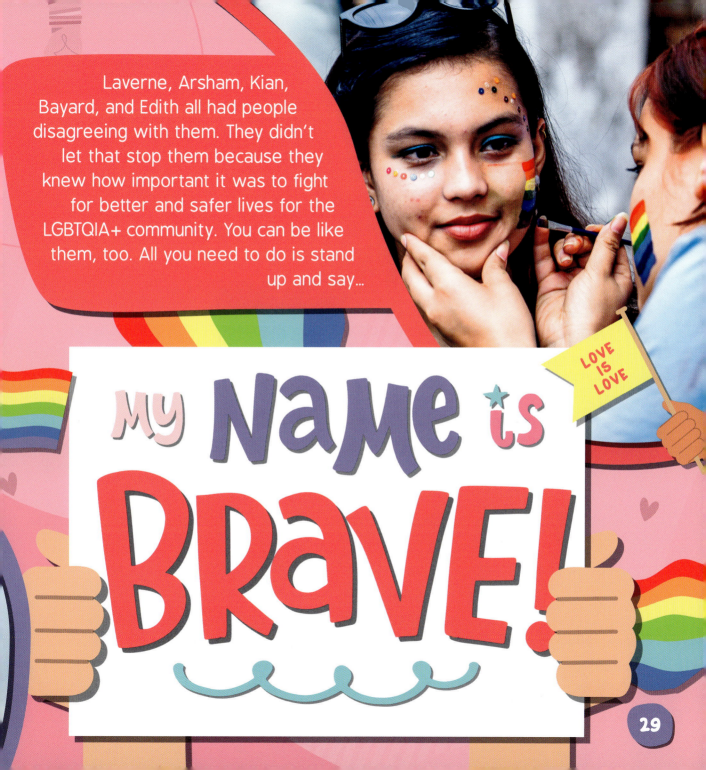

Laverne, Arsham, Kian, Bayard, and Edith all had people disagreeing with them. They didn't let that stop them because they knew how important it was to fight for better and safer lives for the LGBTQIA+ community. You can be like them, too. All you need to do is stand up and say...

MY NAME IS BRAVE!

LOVE IS LOVE

GLOSSARY

aspire to want to have or achieve something

assigned to be given something without having a choice

attracted to want to form a close, romantic, or sexual relationship with someone

awareness knowledge of and understanding about something in the world

biological sex whether a person's sex characteristics are considered to be male, female, or intersex

chromosomes tiny things inside cells (the building blocks that make up all living things) that give our bodies information about what to do and how to grow

cisgender when a person's gender identity matches the biological sex they were assigned at birth

community a group of people who are connected by something

donations things you give in order to help a person or charity, such as food and money

Emmy an award that recognizes excellence in the writing and making of TV shows

feminine things that are stereotypically associated with being female

gender fluid when a person's gender can switch between masculine or feminine or be a mixture of both

genitals parts of the body found between the legs

heterosexual being attracted only to people of the opposite sex

identify to think of yourself as being the same as a particular group of other people

illegal against the law and not allowed

inspired to want to do something because of someone or something else

masculine things that are stereotypically associated with being male

media all the ways that information and entertainment can be passed on to the public, such as TV, movies, newspapers, and radio stations

pansexual when a person can be attracted to anyone regardless of their biological sex, sexuality, or gender

reality the real and true situation that exists

representation acting, speaking, or appearing for a group of people

represents acts as a symbol for something else

sex characteristics physical features that tell you of a person's biological sex

sponsored to be given money to support something

taxes money people pay that allows the government to function

transition to make changes in order to match one's gender identity, often including name, pronouns, clothing, and medical processes

INDEX

A
activism, 5–6, 14

C
charity, 15–17
communities, 6, 9, 12–13, 15, 19–21, 23, 28–29

G
gender, 7–10
governments, 27

I
identity, 7–10

L
laws, 14, 27

M
marriage, 26–27
money, 16–17, 27

P
protests, 5, 22–25

S
schools, 17–19
social media, 19–21

T
transgender, 8, 11, 13, 18–19
TV, 4, 13

V
visibility, 11–13